Thank you to: Elise Jones, who provided the initial spark,
then fanned the flames when they faltered; Matt Shanks for his visionary illustrations;
the students of Fiona White's 2018 Grade Four class at New Gisborne Primary School,
who confirmed I was on the right track; my wife Maggie Millar, who was a constant support;
and last but not least the incredible Secret Scribblers (you know who you are)
who were always there for me in so many important ways. *IHR*

For Marble, the most amazing cat. *MS*

THE MOST AMAZING THING

IAN HAYWARD ROBINSON AND MATT SHANKS

Henry was stuck in the house. He had nothing to do.

He wondered what the others were up to.

His sister, Greta, was doing an experiment.

His father was polishing the lens of his telescope.

His brother, Simon, was sitting on the floor, very still.

His mother was writing her novel.

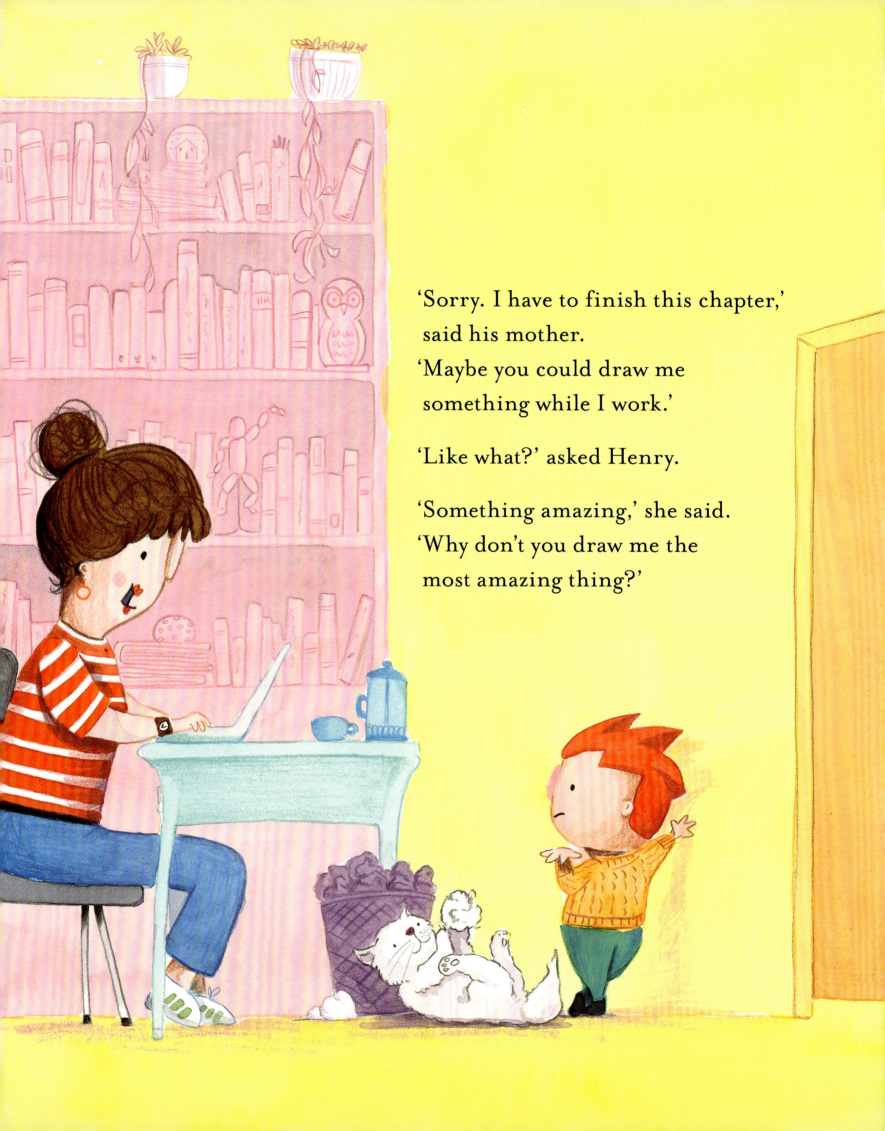

'Sorry. I have to finish this chapter,' said his mother.
'Maybe you could draw me something while I work.'

'Like what?' asked Henry.

'Something amazing,' she said. 'Why don't you draw me the most amazing thing?'

Henry went to his room and got out a big sheet of paper and his coloured pencils.

He stared at the paper. He could not think of anything amazing at all.

He wanted to ask his mother, but she had a sign on her door:

Henry didn't think this was an emergency.

Greta was looking through her microscope.

'Greta,' asked Henry, 'what is the most amazing thing?'

'The most amazing thing is life,' said Greta. 'It is so vibrant and exciting. Look!'

Henry peered through the microscope.

'Each one of those tiny moving blobs is a living creature. Think of all the other living creatures out there – going about their business, full of life.

Life is the most amazing thing.'

Henry didn't feel full of life. He didn't feel very amazing.

Simon was still sitting with his eyes closed.

'Simon,' asked Henry, 'what is the most amazing thing?'

'The most amazing thing is the mind,' said Simon.

'The human mind doesn't just know things.
It also knows that it knows things.
If you know what you know, then you
also know what you don't know,
and your mind starts wondering
and imagining and inventing.
The human mind is the
most amazing thing.'

My mind certainly knows that it doesn't know things, thought Henry. But he didn't feel amazing.

Henry's father was adjusting the controls of his telescope.

'Dad,' asked Henry, 'what is the most amazing thing?'

'The most amazing thing is the universe,' Henry's dad replied.

'It started from a tiny point and exploded into billions of galaxies, each one made up of more stars and planets and moons than we can count. The universe is the most amazing thing.'

Henry tried to picture how huge the universe must be.

This made him feel very small.

And he still wasn't sure what the most amazing thing was.

Henry's mother was taking a coffee break.

'Mum,' said Henry, 'Greta says the most amazing thing is life. Simon says it's the mind. Dad says it's the universe. Which one is it?'

His mother swirled her coffee.

Then she said: 'Those things are all pretty amazing. But I don't think any of them is the most amazing thing.'

'So what IS the most amazing thing?' asked Henry.

'The most amazing thing is you,' Henry's mother said. 'Did you know there is nobody else in the whole world exactly like you? There never has been, and there never will be. You are one of a kind, Henry. YOU are the most amazing thing.'

Henry looked down at himself.

He drew himself up to his full height.

His mind started imagining.

He felt

amazing.

First published by Allen & Unwin in 2024

Copyright © Text, Ian Hayward Robinson 2024
Copyright © Illustrations, Matt Shanks 2024

All rights reserved. No part of this book may be reproduced or transmitted in any form or by any means, electronic or mechanical, including photocopying, recording or by any information storage and retrieval system, without prior permission in writing from the publisher. The Australian *Copyright Act 1968* (the Act) allows a maximum of one chapter or ten per cent of this book, whichever is the greater, to be photocopied by any educational institution for its educational purposes provided that the educational institution (or body that administers it) has given a remuneration notice to the Copyright Agency (Australia) under the Act.

Allen & Unwin
Cammeraygal Country
83 Alexander Street
Crows Nest NSW 2065
Australia
Phone: (61 2) 8425 0100
Email: info@allenandunwin.com
Web: www.allenandunwin.com

Allen & Unwin acknowledges the Traditional Owners of the Country on which we live and work.
We pay our respects to all Aboriginal and Torres Strait Islander Elders, past and present.

 A catalogue record for this book is available from the National Library of Australia

ISBN 978 1 76118 011 8

For teaching resources, explore allenandunwin.com/learn

Illustration technique: watercolour, coloured pencil and acryla gouache

Cover and text design by Sandra Nobes
Set in 22 pt Mrs Eaves OT
Colour reproduction by Splitting Image, Wantirna, Victoria
This book was printed in October 2023 by C&C Offset Printing Co. Ltd, China

1 3 5 7 9 10 8 6 4 2

www.mattshanks.com.au